Pelican Sketchbook

By Julia Frith

I took my sketchbook to the zoo to study the pelicans. I like to draw pelicans because they have an interesting shape.

The pelicans at the zoo live on an island in the middle of a lake, with other water birds.

Each time the pelicans did something new, I tried to draw what they did. I had to draw very quickly and I made notes next to the rough sketches to help me finish the drawing later. It was difficult to get the eyes right.

Sometimes the pelicans stood very still, as though they knew I was drawing them. I looked at their webbed feet with four toes.

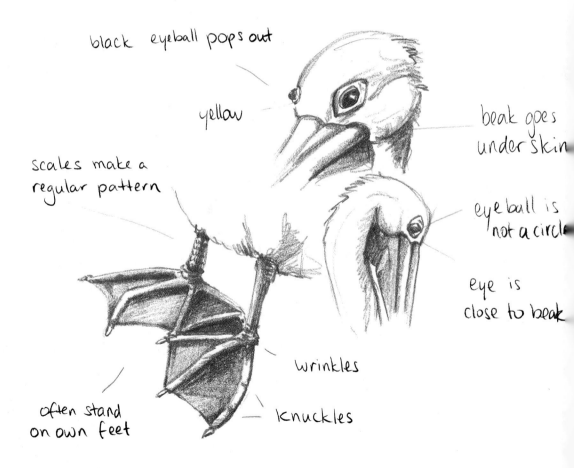

black eyeball pops out

yellow

scales make a regular pattern

beak goes under skin

eyeball is not a circle

eye is close to beak

wrinkles

often stand on own feet

knuckles

The pelican's feet are much better for swimming than for scratching.

I studied the pelicans' beautiful pink beaks, and I watched as the keeper threw fish in the air.

I watched a pelican skim a small fish from just under the surface of the water.

Pelicans catch fish in their bills. A pelican lifts
its head and shuts the top bill down, like a lid.
Then it swallows the fish whole. The keeper
explained how the pouch of the bill stretches,
or billows out under the water like a fishing
net, and the fish is trapped. The pelican lowers
its head to its breast, allowing the water to
drain out. Then the pelican raises its bill high
into the air and swallows the fish head first.

I drew some pelicans sitting on their nests, on the island.

nest close together

nests made from sticks, leaves, feathers.

Pelicans nest near lakes, lagoons or marshes where there are plenty of fish. Some pelicans live near the sea. They build their nests in large groups, or colonies.

It was difficult to draw the chicks.

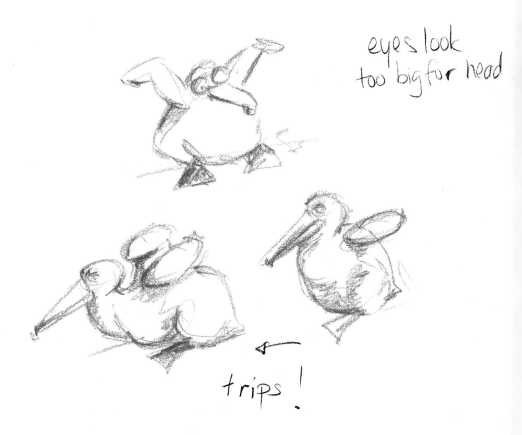

eyes look
too big for head

trips!

Both parents feed the chicks with food from their stomachs. The food looks red and chewed up.

I noticed that the pelicans at the zoo don't often fly away.

You can draw pelicans, too. Look closely at
what they do, and make quick sketches of
what you see. Use a soft pencil, and you may
need an eraser. Write some notes to yourself,
too, about any details you might need to
remember later, when you finish the drawing.

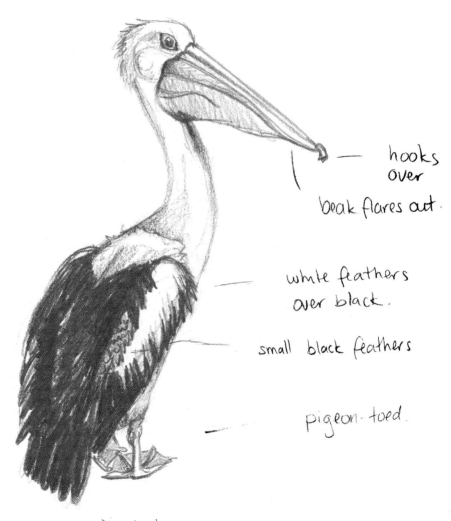

hooks
over

beak flares out.

white feathers
over black.

small black feathers

pigeon-toed.

tail tucks under
wing feathers

Here are some other interesting facts about pelicans:

* When a baby pelican hatches from an egg, it has no feathers. It looks pink and scrawny.

* Groups of baby pelicans are called pods.

* A baby pelican cannot fly until it is about 2 to 3 months old. It stays close to the nest, which is made from a loose gathering of sticks, grass, leaves, and feathers.

* Young chicks can sometimes have violent convulsions that last about a minute. The chick will then collapse. After lying still for about thirty seconds, the chick gets up and behaves normally again. Some zoologists think chicks do this to get their parents' attention!

* Pelicans usually fish in groups of about six or more.

* An adult pelican can weigh from 15 to 30 pounds, and it can have a wingspan of 6 to 9 feet.

* Pelicans often fly in groups. Sometimes they form a v-shape, or they fly in single file, or abreast.

* Pelicans usually fly at heights of around 50 to 100 feet.